Contents

Mirrored love

A time will come

When, with understanding and acceptance

You'll be face to face

With your mind

Soul

Spiritual and physical.

You will all smile,

With wide eyes and stretched out arms

With wine glasses overflowing with love

Drink every last drop.

For this is the love you have been repudiating

The love that knows you best

Your true interests

Face to face with the mirror

The image is now clear

The love you seek

Has always been within.

You Are You

You are you.

Read that again and understand it.

You are God's unrefuted creation. Crafted and blessed by his touch

Alluring in your unique given ways

As daunting as imperfections can be

They make you exclusive from the next

Don't feed into these idealistic commodities that are being sold on these social markets

Don't become a someone else.

Be. You.

Forever be you and no one else, because that's what you have over the world

A special gift that belongs to you and only you. A gift that no one can take from you.

You are you, because every step you take

Every word you speak, every turn you make, every encumbrance you face

No one can handle but you

An empowering ability given to you, don't waste it trying to be somebody else...

Be you.

I Wanna Learn

I wanna learn all about you,
But don't make it easy
Make it a challenge
Make me earn the right to know everything about you
From head to toe
To inside out.

Let me guess your favourite colour
Through trial and error
That way, when I get it right, I feel satisfied
Maybe it's for my pride… but to know that I've figured out something about you…
It's worth it all.

I wanna learn everything about you
But don't make it easy
Keep it a mystery
Make it a challenge
Don't give in or drop your standards
A woman of your beauty and elegance deserves to be fought for.

I wanna know your most interesting fact, your deepest secret

What you fear the most.

What makes you the most happiest and what makes you cry, so I know what's right from wrong.

Your favourite flower,
So I can surprise you
I wanna learn everything about you so I do everything right, and no I'm not perfect and I won't get everything right

But I'll try my best for you.

Intellectual intimacy

Intellectual intimacy

Allow me to foreplay with your mind

Trial and error

Let me discover what excites you

Allow my words to travel through you

Reach parts of your body and soul that have been left untouched

Left unscathed

Let me discover the treasure you possess

With your consent

It would be a honour to explore your sexual anatomy

And If time is money

Let's work overtime

But don't tap out without me

We started together, so we finish together

Let me help you finish off

It will be my pleasure

Teach me all of your best desires

As knowledge is power and you are all I seek.

A Tide of Compatibility & Connections

Moon up, sun down,
We flow peacefully together like the ocean
A taste of your most intimate skin, I now crave.

A fusion of chemicals,
A beautiful reaction not known to the human mind but is accepted by the
heart
Now connected to the point where we think the same and finish each other's...

Sentences, I have plenty.
Endlessly able to describe your mental and physical state
Your gentle and soft touch,
My never ending attraction to every inch of your spirit and soul
I desire daily to get by.

I surrender.
I put down my shields and guards to give you my all
I trust and fear not
Know my all, for you have assured me.

I shall love hard, you've earned it,
Like a flower looking for light, I turn to you
As you are my source of encouragement and hope
An answered prayer, I can never give up.

The growth of me and the future of my name,
Lies within your walls of empowerment.

A perfect gift from God,
A blessing I needed but never thought would happen
In such a short period of time, the memories we have obtained
The growth from a seed to a flower,
I hope we continue to blossom and plant our own seeds.

As days go by and we collect our daily and monthly milestones,
Memories of our every step taken,
Like an apple watch counting our steps
Or like children filled with excitement.

We've grown into people that are compatible for each other,
A strong connection, regardless of the distance apart
We stay connected through ways no other person could comprehend and
that's why I'm certain you were going to be my wife.

Not a needy person,
But a person I have a need for.

Stay...

As you are the queen to my throne
The key to my ever lasting name. The owner of my heart.

Stay with me.

I lost

I lost myself but I didn't give up searching

And in finding myself, I found you

As the sun comes up, I think of you

As the night creeps in, I dream of you

Memories forever on my mind, the taste of your lips forever on mine.

Moon

I am always around

In different shapes, form and presence

Regardless of the distance between us

My alluring soft shine is striking to the defenseless eye

All you have to do is look

During the day, even though it's my time to rest

I stay put

In case you need me at night

I become luminous to guide you home

I stay put to ensure your safety

It is my duty and my sole purpose.

Rain

As I fall to the ground

Listen to how I sound

Allow me to trickle down you

Through your hair, down your spine

Realign your body and mind

Feel reborn

Wash away the burdens

Put out those flames of negativity

As I am here to water the fresh start you desire

As I fall to the ground

Listen to how I sound

At night I set the tone

Relax and smooth

Skin to skin

I feel your every move

As I come to my end

I start to fade away

Promise to not forget about me

I'll return to rain on you again.

These Walls

These walls shiver from past experiences

The cold rainy nights, wash away the scars and traumas

Impossible for me to verbally express

I show my cracks to outline the boarders

The discolouration to paint my emotions

They say time heals

My scars rewind my consciousness...

Still, the wounds on the walls have been rebuilt but the disfigurements remain.

To you, it looks like graffiti

To me, these are my overlaying thoughts

Scattered across from limb to limb, from brick to brick

Maybe someday, someone will pay attention to the detail

Instead of assuming I'm run down or damaged

Still

These walls stand strongly

Impossible to verbally express but now visually able.

I hope you paid attention to my detail.

Contentions

As of late you have provoked me enough

Now I'm screaming with rage

I'm trying to act brave and tough

Even though we both know that it's a bluff

Reciting old traumas like they are your favourite verse

You're trying to hurt me with these cold words like some sort of curse

You're supposed to not hold a grudge and shit

On the phone to your friends, making up lies, that you can't admit

On social media you're posting all these pictures in your best outfits

Trying to lure attention

But it's just building walls of tension

Erupting with words that hold ill intention

And now you've said something that shouldn't even cross your mind

Soul full of anger, we are both blind

Now we haven't spoken for a couple of days

Both stuck in our stubborn ways

Posting all these quotes with white texts on black backgrounds

Trying to understand your thoughts and wrap my mind round

Picking up my phone, putting it down

Thinking it's you,

Every time I hear that text sound

I guess its time to put the pride aside

Come hop in my ride and...

Drown me

Drown me in your love

Be my oxygen, when our lips touch

Inhaling and exhaling

We don't have much time

But I'm glad it's with you

Yearning for your skin

The most beautiful thing

I have seen

Hold me close

In case I fall

Deep into the ocean

Of despair and doubt

In fear of my whereabouts

You show me the truth

My Muse

I dream of you

I can't wait for this

To be my forever view.

Lies of living

High of the essence of lies we call life

I cry

Tears of mixed emotions

Happiness and pain

I wonder what my history is and where my ancestors are from

Concerned by the idea that I may never find out

I guess certain things are not meant to be

Struggling with my mentality

Trying to live on in this world full of lies just to get by.

Social Captivity

My captive mind

projected through my eyes

My surroundings are empty

Humanity on its knees

Told to stay indoors

Now my physical frame is behind my mental gateway

and for once not the other way around

My matters, cycle

From wall to wall

From one place to another

Time after time

A continuum

That we must live by until further notice.

Lonely nights in a pandemic

Days of saying "it's okay"

Turned into months of disarray

Turned into a year of mental decay

I pray throughout the lonely nights

Reminiscent of the day

Taken for granted,

I hope you are all okay

Uncertainties and silent suffering

Suicide rates are doubling

Check up on loved ones

These lonely nights can be deceitful

Probably got their mind full

The need to speak up

But not having the courage to

Offer a helping hand

Or maybe a compliment or two

Be the light that could help someone get through

These lonely nights.

A Queen

A queen who shaped a man, a kind soul

A woman who has lost battles but won wars

A hard worker

Overflowing with confidence

I am in awe

Mind, soul and body serving as one to conquer

Building a world of success, love and beauty

A queen

My inspiration to strive and do well

Possesses the power to develop

To evolve a man who could have been easily led astray

Growing up in an environment of uncertainty

As time went on, I was able to start molding myself

Into an ideal man for myself

A queen who was on the same page as me

Willing to build an empire

Not afraid of the what if's, the but's and the maybe's

Ready to start from the bare minimum of a foundation

To build something incredible

That queen is you

From the moment we met, I knew you was special

Your aura, spirit and energy were divine like a goddess

A goddess of love and war

Now experienced, teach me

Teach me to be the best man for you and I

What makes you smile

What upsets you

What turns you on

What makes your heart beat fast

What takes your breath away

Tell me about your dreams, goals and ambitions

Teach me to be the best father for our children

Help me understand the correct ways

As I only know my father's ways

Not to say my father was absent,

It is just time to evolve

It is time to continue growing

Growing into a man

Fit for a queen like you

Align with your mind

I plan to grow into a man who

Makes you smile in the darkest of times

A man who can pick you up

When you feel knocked down

A man that can calm you down

At your most nervous times

I plan to grow into a man whose

Body and soul have been shaped by a queen that deserves it all

When I'm in your presence

It is like I lose the ability to function

I can do nothing but stare

The reason being is because I don't know how to act

When I'm around a physical gift from God, but can you blame me?

A gift so pure, elegant, alluring, angelic...

A queen.

Nervously Aware

Nervously aware I stare

The level of beauty has caused my hairs to stand up

Goosebumps even

But you're here for me

And I'm here for you

How did we get here...?

I do not know,

But some feelings are still quite blue

Let's start our journey

Destination: Unknown

You go first

I don't want to look crazy or burst

I'll follow your lead

Learn what it's like to be in your need

To touch you in places that's safe and whole

Enjoy what God has crafted

In all your glory

I promise to listen to your story.

Black Lives Matter

Brutality

Losing family members and friends

Attacking the peaceful and the innocent

Causing chaos

Kneeling is no longer enough

Living in constant fear

I wonder how long we will suffer for

Visually watching murderers walk freely

Every life matters you say

Something has to change

May God protect us

After all the pain and hurt

Today we continue to march on

Tomorrow we see another day

Endless fight continues

RIP to all my fallen brothers and sisters.

Pardon me

Pardon me, as I stand here staring bluntly

Unspoken pain, zipped behind these rubber lips

Hundred years of injustice, intertwined into my DNA

The world keeps spinning

Black and white to coloured

We are still fighting for justice

Questioning

History

The real history…

Being told "that was years ago, we should move on"

Yet we still celebrate wearing poppies and told to never forget

Those who lost their lives fighting

But forgotten about the thousands who lost their lives fighting to live.

In time

Hard times

Born into struggle

Building up from rubble

Living in a concrete jungle

You can't tell me what that feels like

I've got to flip a double

Just for as little as a cuddle

To feel welcomed or rewarded

I've concluded that

Being black is not easy but special

Growing up on the estate

Surrounded by detrimental stereotypes

The urge to survive, we are defending various sites

Some smoke that high grade to reach various heights

But I choose to focus on those tunnel lights

Remember to shine bright

It is my time to rise

Spread love, become allies

Shoot for the stars and reach for the skies

Its time

To chase what is mine.

Thank you for reading my book, I hope you thoroughly enjoyed the different journeys portrayed throughout.

For more poetry, follow me on Instagram.

Instagram - Stxvology

Printed in Great Britain
by Amazon